"As our culture collapses around us, the issues of bioethics lie at the heart of its crisis. And why? Because they address the foundational questions of human nature, and every culture is premised on its own assumptions about what it means to be human.

"In this series these extraordinary questions are tackled with due seriousness (they make everyone think) and yet also with accessibility (no one who thinks will be excluded). It is hard to imagine a more important set of questions or a more timely publication."

Nigel M. de S. Cameron, Ph.D.
Provost, Trinity International University

"These booklets are packed with information and moral insights that will provide needed help to pastors, health care professionals, and teachers seeking direction in the ever-changing world of bioethics. Nothing less than human dignity hangs in the balance."

Francis J. Beckwith, Ph.D.
Associate Professor of Philosophy, Culture, and Law
Trinity Graduate School and Trinity Law School
Trinity International University

D0802701

The BioBasics Series provides insightful and practical answers to many of today's pressing bioethical questions. Advances in medical technology have resulted in longer and healthier lives, but they have also produced interventions and procedures that call for serious ethical evaluation. What we can do is not necessarily what we should do. This series is designed to instill in each reader an uncompromising respect for human life that will serve as a compass through a maze of challenging questions.

This series is a project of The Center for Bioethics and Human Dignity, an international organization located just north of Chicago, Illinois, in the United States of America. The Center endeavors to bring Christian perspectives to bear on today's many difficult bioethical challenges. It develops book, audio tape, and video tape series; presents numerous conferences in different parts of the world; and offers a variety of other printed and computer-based resources. Through its membership program, the Center provides worldwide resources on bioethical matters. Members receive the Center's international journal, *Ethics and Medicine*, the Center's newsletter, *Dignity*, the Center's *Update Letters*, special World Wide Web access, an Internet News Service and Discussion Forum, and discounts on most bioethics resources in print.

For more information on membership in the Center or its various resources, including present or future books in the BioBasics Series, contact the Center at:

The Center for Bioethics and Human Dignity
2065 Half Day Road
Bannockburn, IL 60015 USA
Phone: (847) 317-8180 Fax: (847) 317-8153
E-mail: cbhd@banninst.edu

Information and ordering is also available through the Center's World Wide Web site on the Internet: http://www.bioethix.org

BioBasics Series

Basic Questions on
Suicide and Euthanasia

Are They Ever Right?

Gary P. Stewart, D.Min.
William R. Cutrer, M.D.
Timothy J. Demy, Th.D.
Dónal P. O'Mathúna, Ph.D.
Paige C. Cunningham, J.D.
John F. Kilner, Ph.D.
Linda K. Bevington, M. A.

kregel
PUBLICATIONS

Grand Rapids, MI 49501

Table of Contents

Legal Questions

Medical Concerns

Relational Matters

Contributors

Linda K. Bevington, M.A., is the Project Manager for the Center for Bioethics and Human Dignity, Bannockburn, Illinois.

Paige C. Cunningham, J.D., has written numerous articles on abortion and the law; she is a coauthor of the amicus brief that Justice O'Connor cited in her discussion of viability in *Webster v. Reproductive Health Services.*

William R. Cutrer, M.D., served for many years as an obstetrician/gynecologist specializing in the treatment of infertility. He is currently serving as the Dallas/Fort Worth Area Director for The Christian Medical and Dental Society.

Timothy J. Demy, Th.M., Th.D., is a military chaplain and coauthor and author of numerous books and articles. He is a member of the Evangelical Theological Society.

John F. Kilner, Ph.D., is Director of the Center for Bioethics and Human Dignity, Bannockburn, Illinois. He is also Professor of Bioethics and Contemporary Culture at Trinity International University, Deerfield, Illinois.

Dónal P. O'Mathúna, Ph.D., is Associate Professor of Medical Ethics and Chemistry at Mount Carmel College of Nursing, Columbus, Ohio.

Gary P. Stewart, Th.M., D.Min., is a military chaplain and coauthor of numerous books and articles. He is a member of the Evangelical Theological Society.

Introduction

Beliefs have consequences. What we believe about life and death has enormous ramifications for our daily lives. As individuals, families, cultures, and nations, our beliefs regarding the subject of suicide, assisted suicide, and mercy killing are critical. While at times these are three vastly different issues with different demographics and divergent concerns, they all deal with the voluntary taking of human life. They all address pressing needs, such as the relief of suffering and pain. But they all are the wrong response to those needs.

Suicide, assisted suicide, and mercy killing are shortcut attempts to address legitimate concerns. There are, however, better responses to the concerns of the suicidal, of those desiring assisted suicide, and of individuals and societies who must care for them. This book is designed to help you think through these better alternatives. The stakes are high—it is a matter of life and death.

This book is not intended to reproduce all the available information on the subject but rather to simplify, complement, and supplement other available sources that the reader is encouraged to consult. Some of these materials have been listed at the end of this book. This book is not intended to take the place of theological, legal, medical, or psychological counsel or treatment. If assistance in any of these areas is needed, please seek the services of a certified professional. The views expressed in this work are solely those of the authors and do not represent or reflect the position or endorsement of any governmental agency or department, military or otherwise.

1. What is suicide?

At its most basic level, suicide is the act of voluntarily and intentionally killing oneself. Because it is the direct killing of oneself, it is different from indirect, unintentional, and accidental self-death. The word suicide comes from two Latin components, *sui*, meaning "self," and *caedere*, meaning "to kill." Suicide has been studied extensively by many people across the disciplines of medicine, religion, sociology, and psychology. These researchers have not just investigated suicide academically and clinically— they have been personally involved with people who have attempted it. People who attempt suicide typically experience needs of various sorts and are faced with pressing issues for which suicide is perceived as the best "solution."[1] Regardless of how broad or lengthy a definition we construct, the bottom line is that suicide is the desire for, and act of, self murder.

At first glance, both the definition and the act of suicide may appear quite simple. However, the causes and circumstances, the act itself, and the aftermath of suicide are much more complex than is often thought. Suicide elicits many emotions, responses, and reactions in those affected by the death. Words commonly associated with suicide include: anger, discouragement, hopelessness, helplessness, worthlessness, depression, fear, tragedy, mystery, shame, revenge, protest, resentment, release from pain, a search for solutions, a cry for help, a shattered legacy, unanswered questions, unfulfilled dreams, mistakes, desperation, bitterness, hurt, tears, and regrets. Suicide *always* affects many people. Although it presents the illusion of being a solitary act, in reality it has enduring consequences for many.

2. What are some of the myths regarding suicide?

There are many myths and misconceptions regarding suicide. Acceptance of this misinformation can be very detrimental to efforts to recognize and help those who are, or may be, suicidal. All threats, gestures, statements, and conversations about suicide should be taken seriously. If we understand the myths, we will be in a much better position to help others. Here are a few of the most common myths.

- Myth: People who talk about committing suicide do not actually do it.
- Reality: Eighty percent of those who commit suicide have given some indication, especially in verbal statements. Comments such as, "I can't see any way out" or, "You'll be sorry when I'm gone" are definite red flags.

- Myth: Suicidal people are fully intent on dying or are certain to commit suicide.
- Reality: Most people who are suicidal are undecided about living or dying, and they gamble with death, leaving it to others to save them. Relatively few people commit suicide without letting someone know how they are feeling. The final act most often takes place in isolation, but the circumstances leading up to it often are not. Most suicidal people do not want death; they only want to stop what they

consider to be unbearable emotional pain or psychological distress. Nevertheless, there are quite a few cases where signs of a potential suicide are intentionally kept from those close to a suicidal person. When people actually believe that they want or need to die, they often shut out the world around them. Sometimes they leave a suicide note, other times they do not.

- Myth: Once suicidal, always suicidal.
- Reality: Most people are only suicidal for a limited period of time. Feelings change with circumstances, and suicidal thoughts often pass with time as the events causing the despair change or are resolved. Certainly this is not the case with all suicidal people, but it is for many.

- Myth: People who make one suicide attempt will not make subsequent attempts.
- Reality: Most people do not attempt suicide more than once, but 10 percent of those who make an attempt will eventually succeed in committing suicide.

- Myth: Suicide is an act of impulse with no previous planning.
- Reality: Most suicides are carefully planned or considered for weeks before the act. This is certainly not an absolute, however. Every suicide has its own peculiarities, but the norm involves considerable forethought before an attempt.

- Myth: People considering suicide are unwilling to seek help.

- Reality: More than half of those who commit suicide will have received medical care or counseling within the six months preceding the act.

- Myth: Improvement means the risk of suicide is over.
- Reality: Most suicides occur within the first months following the beginning of improvement. Often in the midst of the crisis, the individual does not have the emotional energy to perform the act. However, once there has been some improvement, the individual may attempt or commit suicide to avoid "ever being that low again" or "ever going through that again."

- Myth: Women only threaten suicide, but men accomplish it.
- Reality: Both women and men threaten, attempt, and complete the act of suicide. Suicide is not a gender-specific problem, nor is there a "suicide gene." It is an equal-opportunity crisis for individuals. It is true that five times as many men as women commit suicide and twice as many women as men make suicide gestures and attempts, but suicide seriously affects both genders.[2]

- Myth: If you ask a person directly, "Are you suicidal?" you will prompt a suicide attempt.
- Reality: Asking a person directly about a suicidal intent or inclination will often relieve anxiety the individual has about his or her feelings and may thereby act as a deterrent to suicidal behavior. Communication helps rather than hurts.

- Myth: Only certain types of people commit suicide; others are completely immune from it.
- Reality: Under extremely strenuous or tragic circumstances or a combination of these, *anyone is susceptible to suicide*. It is true that there are risk factors and profiles for individuals who are especially prone to suicide. However, we cannot know with certainty how we will respond to the many trials, traumas, and temptations of life. For some people, suicide might be very unlikely, but it is never impossible.

The myths of suicide are many and have arisen for a variety of cultural reasons. It is extremely important that we all recognize and separate the facts from the fiction of suicide. It crosses all geographic, racial, gender, religious, cultural, and social lines. None of us should underestimate its devastating effects and reach.

3. *Why do people commit suicide?*

There is no single answer as to why people kill themselves. Anyone who has lost a friend or loved one to suicide painfully faces the question "Why?" innumerable times after the death. People who commit suicide have an overwhelming feeling of helplessness, hopelessness, and worthlessness. There are many circumstances and events that can serve as the catalyst for a suicide, and frequently, as we will see later, suicide is a complex matter. People who commit suicide often mistakenly believe that it does not matter if they live or die, that no one will miss them, that friends and family will be better off without them, and that suicide is the only possible way to escape their unbearable emotional pain. For most suicidal people, the goal is not death, but stopping emotional pain. Comments like, "It hurts so much," "I can't stand it any longer," and "I just want peace" are common with those who are suicidal. Ultimately, *suicide is not about death but about living*. It is about an accumulation of our fears and unwanted circumstances that eventually leads to emotional and psychological tunnel vision.

What are some of the emotional trip wires or triggers that precipitate suicide? They are varied and are seldom solitary events or feelings. Often they are a series of unresolved events and feelings that eventually become too great of a burden to carry alone. Among them are depression, alcoholism, substance abuse, anger, revenge, illness, physical infirmity, loss of a loved one, loss of a close friend, loss of a job or other financial setback, public humiliation or loss of social status, and schizophrenia or personality disorders. For each of these triggers, or a combination of them, there is an apparent and ever-*growing* inability to alleviate (lessen) the emotional pain. In such cases, suicide seems to be the only means of relief or escape. Suicide is mistakenly seen as a permanent solution to what appears to be an unresolvable personal problem or series of problems. Regrettably, those who choose suicide are either unwilling or unable to see the horrible consequences of their act in the lives of their families and friends. Suicide always creates more pain than it alleviates.

4. What is the difference between cluster suicides and group suicides?

Cluster suicides occur when a number of people

who are demographically similar and live in the same geographic location commit suicide over a relatively short time span.[3] An example of this would be several students at a particular school committing suicide over a period of a few weeks or months. Similar to the cluster suicide is the "copy-cat" suicide in which several suicides of a similar nature occur after a suicide by a prominent public figure. The suicides that closely followed Marilyn Monroe's suicide are typically cited as examples of this phenomenon. Adolescents are especially vulnerable to both the cluster and the copy-cat suicide because imitation and modeling are prevalent behaviors among this group. They are especially likely to copy the dress, speech, mannerisms, and even other more destructive behaviors of their peers and of popular public figures such as rock stars.[4] Because of this, it is very important for parents to understand the dynamics of suicide and to talk with their children if a friend, classmate, or prominent personality commits suicide.

Group suicides occur when two or more people commit suicide at the same time as part of a "friendship pact," religious act, or because of group pressure. A recent example of group suicide is that of the 1997 Heaven's Gate cult suicides in California. Thirty-nine people killed themselves in the belief that a spaceship, which was supposedly behind the approaching Hale-Bopp comet, would deliver them to their salvation once they abandoned their human bodies or "containers." Another group suicide was the Jonestown, Guyana, tragedy in 1978 when 912 members of a religious cult committed mass suicide.

5. What is assisted suicide or physician-assisted suicide?

Assisted suicide, especially physician-assisted suicide, is one of the most emotional and serious issues that society faces today. It is a highly charged subject with enormous moral, religious, political, social, medical, and legal ramifications for every nation and people. Assisted suicide is suicide that occurs when someone either provides the means by which a person ends his or her own life or otherwise enables the suicide to occur. Physician-assisted suicide is when the physician provides that assistance.

How active a role the physician plays in the death varies from case to case. For example, the physician may advise or prescribe a lethal dose of medication for a patient with the knowledge that the patient intends to use it to commit suicide. Or, as in some of the suicides that Jack Kevorkian has assisted, the physician provides people with some device that allows them to kill themselves. In either case, the physician may or may not be present at the moment of the self-killing. Of course, the people who assist in suicides need not be physicians, that is, they may be pharmacists, nurses, other health-care professionals, friends, or family members. The end is still the same. People are helping other people to kill themselves. Throughout the remainder of this booklet, the term "physician-assisted suicide" will represent all forms of assisted suicide since it is the most discussed form.

6. Why do people consider physician-assisted suicide?

Physician-assisted suicide occurs under circumstances different from most of those noted above, with the exception of depression, illness, and infirmity. There may be several reasons why a terminally-ill person considers or chooses physician-assisted suicide. The issue of *how* we die is as important as the fact *that* we die. Physician-assisted suicide is sometimes promoted as a means by which people can "die with dignity." They want to avoid being subjected to a slow and painful death, surrounded by unwanted medical technology in a sterile environment of a hospital. Many dying people may be disposed to choose physician-assisted suicide because of a fear of losing control of their lives as the illness progresses and death approaches. One result of the tremendous advances in medicine and medical technology in the last couple of decades is that patients and their families now face more options and more end-of-life decisions than previously imaginable. Medical progress has pushed us to new and more complex personal and ethical horizons.

Fear of uncontrolled pain is a significant concern for those who are terminally ill. Once patients receive and understand the diagnosis of incurability, new critical concerns arise. "Awareness of their approaching death compels them to redefine life in stark and unacceptable terms, and the prospect of dying in unrelieved pain becomes a dominant concern."[5] Some of medicine's greatest advances in recent years have been in the field of pain management and any shift to acceptance of physician-assisted suicide undermines the need to pursue further advances. An extremely high degree of effective pain control is presently achievable. Dr. Matthew Conolly notes of cancer pain management, "Our goal is not to provide relief in the form of a morphine-induced fog, but to provide maximal pain relief with minimal side effects."[6]

Thus, fear of unrelieved pain need not prevail. Proper pain management is crucial in deterring those who consider physician-assisted suicide as an option and can be one of the greatest antidotes for the acceptance of physician-assisted suicide.

Depression and fear of isolation can also be heavy factors in the mind-set of those who desire physician-assisted suicide. The fear of isolation is one reality that can be averted through proper care, true compassion, and, if desired, hospice care. Such care permits the terminally ill to die well.

The concern over becoming a financial or other burden can also be a factor in causing people to seek physician-assisted suicide. The lack of sufficient health insurance and the tremendous costs of health care can be major factors in the decision-making process for the terminally ill and their families. Yet even adequate health care may not resolve all of a patient's concerns.

Even when patients have access to sufficient health care, including effective pain management, there can be serious, unmet needs. There can, for instance, be significant suffering, which goes beyond physical pain. Physicians may be effective in meeting patients' physical needs. However, they rarely have the time available to meet the needs of the whole person— including body, mind, and spirit—not to mention the needs of the family.[7]

The needs of the dying are many and should not be downplayed, denied, or ignored. The combination of aggressive involvement, attention, and care by family, friends, and the medical and religious communities can do much to diminish the fears of the dying and their desire for physician-assisted suicide. Such care should never be viewed as optional but as a medical and moral mandate.

7. Is physician-assisted suicide a moral option?

Normally when we talk about physician-assisted suicide, it is in relation to a person who is terminally ill and seeks aid in ending his or her life. Once that case is allowed, however, the acceptability of ending life-not-to-be-considered-worthwhile will extend to other cases. There is a slippery slope here on which respect for human life increasingly loses its footing. As one critic has observed: "Legalizing assisted suicide, even for the consenting terminally ill, will directly threaten the lives of ever increasing numbers of vulnerable people: the physically and mentally handicapped, the aged, the poor, even those whose suffering may only be temporary."[8] Sadly, there is well documented historical evidence to justify this concern (see discussions of Nazi Germany in question 37 and compare with present-day Holland in question 29).[9]

Although physician-assisted suicide is still widely opposed, regrettably, support for it is growing and is rapidly undermining the historical consensus of twenty-five thousand years. A survey by the *Washington Post* found that more than half of those polled said physician-assisted suicide should be legal for those with a terminal illness.[10] The *New England Journal of Medicine* recently reported that one-third of physicians surveyed stated they would write prescriptions for deadly doses of drugs and one-quarter would give lethal injections if physician-assisted suicide was legalized.[11] Professional medicine began in antiquity with the writing of the Hippocratic Oath, in which physicians pledge to give no deadly medicine to anyone if asked. Since that time, the vast majority of physicians have unambiguously been healers; they have worked to promote life rather than helping to cause death. Assent to physician-assisted suicide leads ultimately to the corruption of this role as healer. "Physician-assisted suicide turns the healers into death-dealers, charged with the role of judging someone's quality and quantity of life. The only guide will be their own very fallible judgment.[12]

It is because we *do* care, not because we don't care or don't have compassion for those with great pain or terminal illness, that we must not acquiesce to physician-assisted suicide. Harvard professor Arthur Dyck amplifies this point by noting five reasons why we should not condone physician-assisted suicide: (1) advocacy for life is undermined or lost; (2) advocacy for pain relief is undermined or lost; (3) limits to physician-assisted suicide are inherently unstable; (4) suicide prevention in general is severely compromised; and (5) informed choice is an inadequate safeguard.[13] Physician-assisted suicide may appear to be compassionate and caring, but ultimately its acceptance will erode societal values as well as end human lives. Its many other implications are detailed in questions 2–5 of this book.

8. What is euthanasia?

The word *euthanasia* is derived from two classical Greek words, *eu* meaning "good" and *thanatos,* meaning "death"; thus, the term literally means "good death." The word refers to the process by which people's deaths are intentionally brought about by themselves or others, sometimes for generally commendable ends such as the relief of pain and suffering. In other words, while some people use the term *euthanasia* only when one person is killed by another (i.e., "mercy killing"), the term is broad enough to also encompass suicide and assisted suicide as well as the withholding of life-sustaining care with the intention of ending a person's life. Euthanasia is not a new concept in Western society, and the morality of it is widely debated today. It is being championed by organizations such as the Hemlock Society, EXIT, and Choice in Dying. The slogans, definitions, and terms surrounding euthanasia are confusing and deceptive. Some of the most common phrases used in discussions of the subject are *active euthanasia, passive euthanasia, voluntary euthanasia, involuntary euthanasia,* and *nonvoluntary euthanasia.* Questions 9 and 10 will sort out these various terms.

9. What is the difference between active and passive euthanasia?

Discussions of euthanasia are often unproductive because of confusion over definitions. Consider, for example, the various types of euthanasia. The terms *active euthanasia* and *passive euthanasia* refer to the *kind* of involvement others have in ending a person's life. Active euthanasia is the effort of a person to cause his or her own death or the death of another. In all three forms of active euthanasia—suicide, assisted suicide, and mercy killing—the medical cause of death is not disease or injury but the fatal action taken. Although people sometimes equate euthanasia only with mercy killing, it is more accurate to distinguish mercy killing from the other two forms of active euthanasia as well as from passive euthanasia (see question 8 and Figure 10–1 at the end of question 10).

Passive euthanasia intends death by withholding (including withdrawing or refusing) available medical treatment or other care that *clearly* could enable a person to live *significantly* longer. Death is intended but not medically caused by the person performing passive euthanasia. Another expression for this practice is "intentionally fatal withholding." Using this expression can be helpful, since it is more explicit about what is in view than is the term *passive euthanasia*. It is important not to confuse intentionally fatal withholding—which is always morally problematic—with legitimately withholding useless treatment, e.g., when death is imminent even with treatment (see *End of Life Decisions* in this series).[14]

In the case of mercy killing (i.e., active euthanasia), the physician usually induces death by injecting a lethal drug into the patient. In the case of intentionally fatal withholding (i.e., passive euthanasia), the physician withdraws treatment already begun (such as a respirator) or decides not to begin treatment (such as cardiopulmonary resuscitation) and lets an *avoidable* death take place. To repeat: The difference between active euthanasia (i.e., mercy killing) and passive euthanasia (i.e., intentionally fatal withholding) is the difference between whether a person or the disease/injury is the medical cause of death.

These categories can be helpful in sorting out what is going on when one speaks of relieving pain. If an overdose of pain medication is given in order to cause death, the death that eventually occurs is euthanasia. If only enough pain medication is given to relieve a dying patient's pain and the patient dies, the death that occurs is not euthanasia. Euthanasia is always the *intent* to bring about someone's death.

10. How are voluntary, involuntary, and nonvoluntary euthanasia different?

These three terms do not apply to suicide or assisted suicide because all acts of self-killing are voluntary; however, they do provide a more precise understanding of mercy killing (active euthanasia) and intentionally fatal withholding (passive euthanasia).

Voluntary mercy killing occurs when a patient requests that someone take his or her life, and his or her desire is honored. *Involuntary* mercy killing occurs when a patient explicitly refuses to be killed, and his or her request is not honored. Finally, *nonvoluntary* mercy killing occurs when a patient is killed by someone who is not aware of the patient's wishes, either because those wishes are unobtainable or because the person chooses not to obtain them.

Two questions can be asked to determine which type of mercy killing (active euthanasia) is being performed. First, ask: "Do I know if the patient wishes to be killed based on his or her oral or written statement?" If the answer is no and the patient is killed, the death is nonvoluntary mercy killing. If the answer is yes and the patient is killed, the death is either voluntary or involuntary mercy killing. Second, to determine whether voluntary or involuntary mercy killing is involved, ask: "Am I acting in accordance with the wishes of the patient?" If the answer is no and the patient is killed against his or her wishes, the death is involuntary mercy killing. If the answer is yes and the patient is killed in accordance with his or her wishes, the death is voluntary mercy killing.

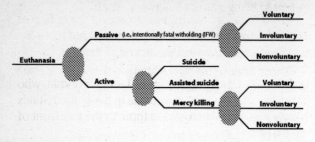

These same two questions can be asked to determine what type of intentionally fatal withholding (passive euthanasia) is involved.

Although voluntary mercy killing and intentionally fatal withholding are morally unacceptable (see questions 14–22), the involuntary and nonvoluntary forms of these are particularly heinous. These forms of euthanasia involve assuming *total* responsibility for another's very existence—a responsibility that no one can rightly assume.

11. What lies behind the increasing openness to euthanasia, especially physician-assisted suicide?

The tragedy of euthanasia lies in the generally well-intentioned arguments that people use to justify it. "They boil down to two ideas: respect for autonomy (*It's my life; let me decide how and when to end it*) and compassion (*I wouldn't want to suffer like that* or, as we often put it, *I wouldn't let my dog go through this—we'd take him to the vet*)."[15] While these are deeply deceptive arguments, they appeal to the values that we hold dear. Each of them will be addressed later, but it's easy to understand their appeal at first hearing.

The increasing willingness to accept the option of euthanasia, especially in the form of physician-assisted suicide, is also one of the results of the increased secularization of our society in the last few decades. Certainly the actions of Jack Kevorkian, who has assisted in dozens of suicides in the United States since 1990, have brought the topic to the forefront of the daily news and people's thinking.

Interestingly, Derek Humphrey, a longtime activist for euthanasia and physician-assisted suicide, believes that the euthanasia movement has gained momentum in recent years because of the abortion issue and *Roe v. Wade,* the United States Supreme Court case legalizing abortion, which he identifies as the turning point in society's openness to euthanasia. When the "right to choose" to terminate a pregnancy and kill the unborn baby became legal (founded on the premise of the "right to privacy"), the euthanasia movement gained new energy. Once the privacy principle was legally established in the *Roe* case so as to allow the taking of innocent human life, it became increasingly difficult, if not impossible, to brake the descent. A momentum has been established in which the former presumption in favor of human life has given way to many forms of rationalization and excuses for the taking of human life.[16]

Euthanasia advocates take every possible opportunity to identify their cause with that of the pro-choice side of the abortion debate. They believe that by coupling euthanasia as the caboose to abortion's locomotive, they can benefit the euthanasia cause and gain the same public acceptance for euthanasia that they perceive currently exists for the right of a woman to terminate her pregnancy.[17]

In a morally relativistic society that rejects the existence of any absolutes, the ever-changing values of society and popular opinion will determine all decisions, including those involving life and death. As we will see later, the Christian message of hope, with its view of life and death, is vastly different. "In making clear to the whole of society what Christian teaching offers in an affirmative way, we may be able to slow or reverse our society's current descent into the moral maelstrom that Pope John Paul II has recently called the 'culture of death.'"[18]

12. Is euthanasia a moral option?

Proponents of euthanasia claim that death can be "natural" and "good" if its manner and timing can be controlled. However, the Christian view of death is far different. It holds that the philosophical concept of a "good" death is a contradiction of terms. People may indeed die with little pain or suffering, and they may die gently and well, but death itself is never good. There is nobility and dignity in caring for the dying but not in dying itself. Dying separates loved ones from one another and individuals from the larger community. The idea that dignity is well-served by such separation is to misunderstand dignity. Dignity is rooted in life—how we live and care for one another. It is death that is the indignity because it is something that is completely alien to God's design and desire for humanity. It is something that is imposed upon humanity as a consequence of our sin and separation from God.[19]

For Christians, death is an aberration of God's original plan and is inconsistent with their eternal destiny in Christ. We must have compassion for and care for the dying, but we must not hasten or assist in their deaths. Edmund Pellegrino summarizes this outlook well.

On the Christian view, a dignified death is one in which the suffering person takes advantage of all the measures available to relieve pain and ameliorate the things that cause a loss of imputed dignity but also recognizes that his or her innate dignity remains. In a dignified death, we affirm ourselves as persons by giving ourselves over to God's presence even in our most despairing moments, just as Jesus did in the awful hours of Gethsemane and Golgotha. Paradoxically, the death by crucifixion was, for the Romans who crucified Jesus, the most undignified of deaths. Yet, in the way Jesus confronted crucifixion, it became the most dignified death the world has ever experienced.[20]

A Christian view of life and death rejects euthanasia but energetically promotes care and compassion for the dying. "In relating to the sick, the suffering, the incompetent, the disabled, and the dying, we must learn again the wisdom that teaches us *always to care, never to kill.* Although it may sometimes appear to be an act of compassion, killing is never a means of caring."[21] We can and must practice both caring without coercion and compassion without killing. Proper pain management, compassionate treatment, and hospice care, when and if needed, are forms of caring currently available for those in the valley of the shadow of death.

13. How common are suicide, physician-assisted suicide, and euthanasia?

Suicide is on the increase in developed countries where national statistics are tracked.[22] In 1995, suicide was the ninth leading cause of death in the United States, accounting for 1.3 percent of total deaths.[23] In the United Kingdom, figures were lower, but still significant.[24] In the United States, approximately thirty thousand suicides are reported each year (some researchers have estimated a figure more than double that and perhaps three to five times as much because many suicides are unreported officially).[25] What else do we know? Here's a quick glimpse:

- Suicide by firearms is the most common method for both men and women, accounting for sixty percent of all suicides.
- Nearly eighty percent of all firearm suicides are committed by Caucasian males.
- Twice as many women as men report that they have attempted suicide.
- Four times as many men than women die by suicide.
- Seventy-three percent of all suicides are committed by Caucasian males.
- The highest suicide rates are for persons over sixty-five years of age.
- Suicide is the third leading cause of death among young people fifteen to twenty-four years of age (including six times as many males as females).
- There are an estimated eight to twenty-five attempted suicides for every completed suicide (240,000 to 750,000 annually in the United States).
- The strongest risk factors for attempted suicide in youth are depression, alcohol, and drug use.[26]

From the information above, we can see that more women attempt suicide than men but that men are more likely to accomplish the act. In the United States, though their numbers are small, Native Americans have the highest rate of suicide, followed by Caucasians, Japanese Americans, Chinese Americans, Hispanics, African Americans, and Filipino Americans.[27] For all concerned, these facts and figures are troubling and strongly suggest that no suicidal remark or attempt be considered insignificant or insincere.

Exact figures for physician-assisted suicide and euthanasia are difficult to determine because of the legal prohibitions against them. With the exception of the Netherlands, where both practices are illegal but widely tolerated, figures are almost nonexistent. One government-sponsored study in the Netherlands found that in 1990, 1.8 percent of all deaths, or about 2,300 were caused by physicians acting on their patients' orders. However, it also found that an additional 1,040 people were put to death by their physicians without consent.[28] The study, known as the Remmelink Report, also showed that 8,100 patients died from an intentional overdose of morphine or other pain-control medications given primarily to terminate life. If euthanasia and physician-assisted suicide were legal in the United States and we were to extrapolate equivalent percentages for the three Dutch figures above, it would mean that there would be 41,500 acts of euthanasia, 16,000 involuntary deaths by physicians, and 78,000 intentional overdoses resulting in deaths (see also, question 29).[29]

In the absence of legal protection, current actual figures are undoubtedly lower but difficult to establish.

A recent national survey of physician-assisted suicide and euthanasia in the United States reports that 6 percent of physicians, those most likely to receive a request for a lethal prescription or injection, complied with the request of their patients (i.e, 114 of 1,902 who responded). This is the result while physician-assisted suicide is still illegal. It is interesting to note that physicians were surveyed "during a time when medical education in palliative care [pain medication] was largely unavailable and such care was sporadically delivered."[30] As palliative care becomes more available, such requests may hopefully diminish.

THEOLOGICAL ISSUES

14. How does my view of God affect my understanding of taking human life?

How do you view God? The answer is very important because the way a person views God and the quality of the relationship with God will be significant factors in how one deals with stress and crisis. Throughout the Psalms, we read of the human emotions that accompany the broad spectrum of circumstances in the psalmists' and our own lives. There we find joy and sadness, fear and pain, exuberance and depression, victory and defeat, hope and despair. The emotions expressed in the Psalms are as diverse as the events that generated them. What sustained the writers throughout the course of these events was personal faith and a biblical worldview—the ability to view life in accordance with God's divine perspective (see Pss. 102, 116, and 121). These same supports are available to us today.

When life's inevitable traumas, catastrophes, and crises threaten to cast us violently upon destructive rocks and shoals, it is personal faith and our worldview (which includes our view of God) that chart the way to safety. Knowing God as the Who behind our circumstances enables us to move beyond the why of our circumstances. Such knowledge doesn't deny the circumstances or the pain and suffering we may endure, but it does help give perspective to them. Our fears and tears are very real, but knowing God and understanding something of God's nature can lead us from despair to hope.

The Bible teaches us that God is omniscient and omnipresent, that is, all-knowing and everywhere. God knows all actual and possible things. God knows the anguish and anxiety in each of our lives and is aware of every aspect of our daily existence. God is also present in the midst of our trials and temptations, which means we are never alone or helpless, even though our feelings would have us believe otherwise (see Ps. 139). Scripture also teaches that God is omnipotent or all powerful. God is able to deliver us from all of our trials and temptations, including suicide. The Bible also affirms the loving character of God. God's love for each of us is so great that Jesus Christ died for us. There is a depth to God's love that we will never be able to comprehend fully. *God is greatly concerned for us, cares deeply for us, and loves us more than we will ever know.* The intense self-focus of the suicidal individual and the limited human perspective of those who would assist in suicide ignore or underestimate God's active love and

33

concern. The difficulties we face in life are very real but so also is the loving God to whom we can take them. We are *never* alone.

15. How does human dignity relate to the taking of human life?

From a Christian perspective, humanity's distinctiveness is found in one indisputable theological fact: Every individual is created in the image of God. Each and every human being has innate, intrinsic, and immeasurable significance precisely because each is a human being. Therefore, the taking of life and the conditions under which it is taken must be seriously and scrupulously considered. A Christian view of humanity recognizes the foundational dignity of all people.

For Christians, human dignity resides in the fact that a person is a creature of God and has value simply because he or is a person and not because others attribute dignity to him or her. Human dignity, therefore, can never be lost, even when one is diminished in one's own eyes or the eyes of others, even when one is shunned because of one's appearance, incontinence, or pain. A human person is a creature for whom God chose to die. How can such a creature lose his or her God-given dignity?[31]

Human dignity is not diminished by illness or circumstances, though such a thought is a common mistake when people are in the midst of extreme pain and illness. In particular, we must resist the temptation to relieve *our own* frustrations and bitterness over the prolonged deaths of others by pretending that we can kill them to sustain *their dignity.*[32]

Recognizing that humanity is created in the image

of God has far-reaching personal, theological, and cultural implications, including the rejection of euthanasia in all of its forms. To ignore the Creator God and His purpose for creating humanity in general, and every individual in particular, is to miss the fact that we exist for a purpose beyond ourselves and that we, therefore, do not have the right to abandon our own lives or the lives of others to premature death.

16. Are there any instances of suicide in the Bible?

Six suicides are recorded in the Bible, five in the Old Testament and one in the New Testament.[33] In none of the cases is there a moral approval of the act. Rather, there is merely a recording of the events. The Bible never denies historical events or belittles human emotions. It faithfully presents the good and bad experiences of life. Murder, adultery, theft, lying, anger, and suicide are all reported in the pages of the Bible. Such reports are part of the reason that Scripture is so meaningful and applicable to us today. Its accounts mirror the events and emotions of our own day.[34]

The first instance of suicide in the Bible is that of Abimelech, the son of Gideon. When wounded in battle, Abimelech commanded his aide to hasten his death by killing him (Judg. 9:50–55). In 1 Samuel 31:1–6, we find the suicidal death of Saul, king of Israel. As was Abimelech, Saul also was wounded in battle and asked his armor bearer to kill him. When the man refused, Saul drew his own sword and fell on it. But Saul may well not have died from this self-inflicted wound. Scripture records an Amalekite's claim to have killed Saul. He tells King David that he came upon Saul after Saul had mortally wounded himself with his sword. In his agony, Saul implored the Amalekite to have mercy on him and kill him. Knowing that Saul's death was imminent, the Amalekite honored Saul's request and killed him. David's response is instructive. Reflecting the biblical perspective that human life is precious, he finds the Amalekite's action not to be compassionate but offensive and worthy of severe punishment (2 Sam. 1:1–16). When Saul's armor bearer sees that his king is dead, he commits suicide in his despair (1 Sam. 31:5).

The fourth instance of suicide is the death of Ahithophel, advisor to David and Absalom. His death is recorded in 2 Samuel 17:23, where we read that when his counsel was not received by Absalom, he "saddled his donkey and arose and went to his home, to his city, and set his house in order, and strangled [hanged] himself." Old Testament scholar Dr. Eugene Merrill notes of this suicide, "Ahithophel's suicide, triggered by his public humiliation, is no spur-of-the-moment deed—he thinks through his options and concludes that self-destruction is his best."[35]

The final suicide recorded in the Old Testament is that of Zimri, who was king of Israel for seven days and who burned his palace, killing himself (and probably others) rather than be captured by his enemies (1 Kings 16:18). In these five instances, it is important to note that none of the suicides is viewed favorably or viewed as a legitimate option, even in the most difficult of times.[36]

One suicide is recorded in the New Testament— that of Judas Iscariot, who hanged himself after betraying Jesus (Matt. 27:3–10; Acts 1:18–19). Some advocates of suicide have contended that Paul's intense desire to be with the Lord, as recorded in Philippians 1:21–26, was a latent suicide desire. Such an interpretation misses Paul's main point. Contemplating eternal life with God should lead to a greater desire to serve the Lord in this life (2 Cor. 5:9; Rom. 14:7–8). In Philippians 1:19–26, Paul does acknowledge that death can look very attractive. But Christians should resist that temptation, as he did, and find ways to love others and glorify God.[37]

17. Do I have a "right to die"?

Much of the contemporary rhetoric in suicide debates involves either the affirmation or the denial of the right to die.[38] How valid is the concept? The central ideas of the right-to-die philosophy come from the concepts of the primacy of autonomy and the self-determination of the individual: "*My* life is my own and I alone have the right to determine how it is (or is not) lived." Over the past three decades, the right to die has come to mean not only that the patient should be allowed to die (by withdrawing treatment) but that he or she has the right to be dead.[39] Advocates of this right "claim not only a right to attempt suicide but a right to succeed, and this means, in practice, a *right to the deadly assistance of others.* It is thus certainly proper to understand the 'right to die' in its most radical sense, namely, as a right to become or be made dead, by whatever means."[40]

Yet, the very concept of a right to die is contrary to the entire history of rights in the last three centuries. Both philosophically (especially in terms of political theory) and legally, a right to die is nonexistent. As one scholar observes, "If we start at the beginning, with the great philosophical teachers of natural rights, the very notion of a right to die would be nonsensical."[41] All rights, he explains, presuppose our self-interested attachment to our own lives. All natural rights are rooted in the primary right to life, or more specifically, the right to self-preservation.

Three of the major dangers of accepting a right-to-die attitude mirror broader problems with the increasing openness to euthanasia:

First, the right to die, especially as it comes to embrace a right to "aid-in-dying," or assisted suicide, or euthanasia, will translate into an obligation on the part of others to kill or help kill.

Second, there can be no way to confine the practice to those who knowingly and freely request death. The vast majority of persons who are candidates for assisted death are, and will increasingly be, incapable of choosing and effecting such a course of action for themselves.

Third, the medical profession's devotion to healing and refusal to kill—its ethical center—will be permanently destroyed, and with it, patient trust and physician self-restraint.[42]

The slogan, "the right to die," contains the subtle suggestion of "the obligation to die." We as individuals and a culture must draw a line in the sand and say no. Rather than a right to die, we have an obligation to live. If we truly care for ourselves and others as people and patients, then we must reject the right-to-die euphemism and its false promise that we can aid the person by eliminating the person.[43]

18. Is it wrong for me to want to die?

This is a very serious question that touches on many issues. The circumstances under which the question is asked are different for the relatively healthy person who is contemplating suicide and for the person who is terminally ill or has an extremely painful and debilitating condition. The answer is not simply yes or no. The answer must be given in extended conversation with the individual who is asking the question. The desire for death may be understandable but should not dictate our actions.

Death does not terminate our personal existence. We are more than flesh and blood, and the deterioration of the body does not mean we cease to be persons. According to the Bible, death will entail, for the unbeliever, a far more painful conscious separation from God than any end-of-life suffering that is involved (Dan. 12:2; Matt. 25:41–46; Luke 16:19–31; Rev. 20:11–15). Love for unbelievers should motivate us to be sure that they do not naïvely seek death without knowing what it will entail. Albeit, a Christian knows that to be physically dead is to be in heaven with Christ—an existence far better than anything this world has to offer. That's why Paul could say "to die is gain" (Phil. 1:21). But he attaches to that thought the recognition that "to live is Christ," i.e., to live under the lordship of Christ in the service of others. As Paul goes on explicitly to conclude that what comes after death for the believer is something to look forward to, the decision to die is not for us to make. We are to leave the timing of our deaths in God's hands.

The desire for death can be very strong in some people, and that desire should be addressed. We should ask those who express a desire to die, "Why do you desire death?" Is it because of humiliation, discouragement, intractable pain, fear, or a host of other catalysts? Once we understand the desire, we can address it appropriately.

For the terminally ill individual, there is an important difference between the desire to die and the recognition and acceptance that death is unavoidably imminent. People have no obligation to endure treatment that will not benefit them. Care for the terminally ill always falls on a continuum, with the possibility of overtreatment being at one end and the possibility of undertreatment at the opposite end. Neither is desirable and thus careful decisions must be made by the patient, family, and caregivers.[44] There is a crucial difference between accepting death and intending death. The former is permissible, the latter is not. We cannot avoid some evils in this world, death being but one of them. We are to accept death when we can no longer forestall it, rejoicing in the knowledge that God will bring us a greater good through it. But if circumstances give us the opportunity to continue to live, then we are not to choose (i.e., intend) death, either by medically causing it or fostering it by forgoing available treatment.[45]

In the case of the suicidal individual, for whom death is not imminent due to illness, acting upon a desire for death is wrong for many of the same reasons that apply in the case of one who is terminally ill. Life is a gift from God, and our lives are not truly our own (1 Cor. 6:19–20). Even though death can look very attractive, it must not be pursued. We are given life as a stewardship, and we are to use life to serve others rather than self. Suicide does not make life better for others. It produces long-lasting hurt and other consequences that affect family and friends for many years and even generations. A suicidal desire for death is a cry for help. If you hear the cry, respond; if the cry is your own, please seek help.

19. Should suffering be eliminated at all costs?

As we think about the concept of suffering, we must distinguish between pain, which we normally think of as primarily physiological, and suffering, which is a broader concept that encompasses pain as well as other medical, social, familial, and theological factors. Although the words are often used interchangeably in casual conversations, it is not wise to do so.

Pain management and suffering management may be two different things. Certainly we need to control pain, and great progress has been made in this field. In the majority of cases, pain can be controlled. Indeed, striving to maximize the patient's quality of life by alleviating pain is essential. The goal is not to provide relief in the form of a drug-induced fog but to provide maximal pain relief with minimal side effects. More education and research need to be done. As anesthesiologist Dr. Matthew Conolly concludes, "Where death is inescapable, conquest of pain is the last great service that we can render to our patients, and it is important that we succeed."[46]

Suffering, however, involves more than physical pain. It can also include a host of feelings such as fear, abandonment, isolation, despair, and loss. For example, a parent who loses a child may be said to suffer even though the parent is not hurting physically. The alleviation of suffering therefore encompasses more than medical treatment. It calls for a response of family, friends, church, health-care professionals, and the community. Suffering is to some degree a unique experience for every individual.[47] To respond adequately to suffering, we must sort out the many issues involved, medical and otherwise.

While we may not fully understand the causes or purposes of suffering, there is an appropriate Christian response to it, and we can grow spiritually from it. This is not to say that all suffering is redemptive or that Christians should seek out suffering or prolong it. Christians are called on by biblical standards to relieve pain and suffering when possible. However, because suffering has meaning, even though a mysterious one, Christians can offer something more than extinction to the suffering person.[48] They can offer the hope of eternal life, where there will be no pain or suffering, no tears or tragedy (Rev. 21:4). The Christian can also offer the certainty that the cries of the sufferer do not go unheard. The sufferings of Jesus Christ, God incarnate, who suffered and died for our redemption, make this great hope and assurance available to all who accept His offer of salvation (Heb. 4:15–16; 12:1–2).

We must do what we can to eliminate both pain and suffering. Great compassion and care are required of all involved, including the community at large. To be genuinely compassionate, we must literally be willing to suffer with another person. Compassion is an emotion that encourages us to identify with the physical, mental, or emotional suffering of another. It is impossible to understand fully and help another person when we separate ourselves from his or her suffering—either by physically and emotionally withdrawing from the person or by killing the person. These are not acts of compassion but abandonment. In the same way that love is not genuine in the context of adultery, so compassion is not genuine in the context of killing. Compassion identifies with human weakness and looks beyond the spiritual or physical condition of a person to provide help. "He, being compassionate . . . did not destroy them. . . . He remembered that they were but flesh, a wind that passes and does not return" (Ps. 78:38–39). Compassion honors life in every way; it does not ever hasten death (see Matt. 9:36; 14:14; 15:32; 18:27; 20:34; and Mark. 6:34 on the life of Jesus). To eliminate suffering by eliminating sufferers is to shirk one's responsibility to pursue genuine compassion. It is to abandon those who suffer—and the God who has pledged to see them through in their time of greatest need.

20. Is suicide the unpardonable sin?

Perhaps you have heard people say that suicide is unpardonable or unforgivable by God. This idea is often based on the belief that the person who commits suicide is unable to ask for and receive forgiveness after the act and, therefore, receives eternal punishment. Indeed, you can't ask for forgiveness after you are dead. Because suicide is self-murder, it is sinful.

The act of suicide does not, however, condemn anyone to eternal punishment and separation from God. Salvation and eternal life are gifts that God freely gives to all who acknowledge their sinfulness to God and trust personally in the death of Christ on the cross as the just payment for their sinfulness (John 3:16; Eph. 2:8–9; Rom. 8:31–33; 2 Cor. 5:21).

Salvation for any person rests in the finished work of Jesus Christ on the cross, not in abstaining from sinful acts. Our committing suicide in and of itself does not condemn us to eternal punishment any more than does any other sin for which we have not asked forgiveness at the time of death (see 1 Cor. 3:9–15;

2 Cor. 5:10). For the Christian, there is no individual act or sin that can erase salvation, change eternal destiny, or separate the believer from God—including suicide (Rom. 8:1, 37–39). We are by our very nature sinful, and any of the many sins we commit throughout our lives would condemn us to separation from God (Rom. 3:23; 6:23) if there was no cross upon which the debt of a believer's past, present, and future sin has been eternally paid. The biblical passages from which the idea of an unpardonable sin is derived, such as Hebrews 6, typically neither have in view an individual sin (action) nor something that is unpardonable. They challenge people who are at risk of faltering in their walk with God to stay in close relationship with God, who is ever faithful to forgive and sustain them. A possible exception is Mark 3:28–30. But even there Jesus emphasizes that *all* sins, except rejecting the redemptive work of the Holy Spirit in one's life, can be forgiven.

Salvation and suicide are two separate issues. We all have committed many sins throughout our lives. We all need salvation, totally apart from the issue of suicide. Each person must choose to accept or reject the death of Jesus Christ for his of her own life.

The destiny of anyone you have known who has already committed suicide was not settled by the act of suicide; it was settled by his or her relationship with Christ. That relationship may have been public or private. Even that person, for any number of reasons, may have been uncertain about it. God, however, is not uncertain as to the identity of His children, so we must rest in His mercy, love, and eternal promises. Suicide is normally a very private act, and what may have transpired spiritually in those final moments of despair is known only to God. God hears the prayers and cries of all who call out, and He is always faithful in answering those petitions.

21. Have Christians always been opposed to suicide?

Throughout the history of Christianity, there has been a rejection of suicide as a viable option for Christians. There are extensive statements by theologians, such as Augustine and Thomas Aquinas, who explicitly call suicide immoral. Across the spectrum of Christian teaching, suicide has been rejected. Whether one looks to history and the teachings of Roman Catholicism, Orthodoxy, or Protestantism, there is a widespread rejection of suicide.

The fact that Christianity has historically rejected suicide does not mean that Christians are or have been immune from suicide. However, as a philosophy, practice, and principle of life, it has little historical support in Christianity. The reason for this consistent opposition is that suicide directly contradicts some of the most basic convictions of the Christian faith. So foundational are the goodness and sovereignty of God in the writings of early church leaders and so consistently do they stress patient endurance of affliction as an essential Christian virtue, that it is not at all surprising that these writings do not refer to suicide at all. As Christians, we are to affirm life in all of its complexities and challenges—not pursue death. As one writer observes:

The Christian prohibition of suicide is clearly based in our assumption that our lives are not ours to do with as we please. But that prohibition is but a reminder of the kind of commitments that make suicide, which appears from certain perspectives and at particular times in our lives so rational, so wrong. It reminds us how important is our commitment to be the kind of people who can care about a sick little girl and in the process learn to care for ourselves. That kind of lesson may not give life meaning, but it is certainly sufficient to help us muddle through with enough joy to sustain the important business of living.[49]

22. Is there a difference between suicide and martyrdom?

Some theologians and historians have recently argued that martyrdom was a form of suicide sought by the early Christians and applauded by the Christian tradition. Such a view, however, distorts history and confuses the motives of the martyred. There is a difference between seeking death and being willing to die. Suicide is an act in which someone *intends* to die; martyrdom is an act in which someone who is *willing* to die for his or her beliefs is killed. In martyrdom there is no intent to die. Whereas martyrdom is the ultimate act of suffering and sacrifice for one's beliefs, suicide typically is the ultimate act of escape from suffering. Suicide in the face of illness can be seen as analogous to martyrdom only if God is viewed either as significantly less than sovereign or as an oppressive tyrant.[50]

The apostles of the early church understood that their commitment to Christ could cost them their lives. The Lord had warned them of the world's hatred of Him and, therefore, its hatred of them (John 15:18–25). In a fallen world, some will pay the ultimate price for proclaiming the truth as Christ Himself did. To compare his or their sacrifice to a suicide is to confuse an act of selfless love with an act of self-centeredness.

LEGAL QUESTIONS

23. How has the law historically viewed suicide?

Much of American law is derived from English law. From at least the thirteenth century, England viewed suicide as a serious felony, calling it homicide. Suicide was seen as an offense against the Crown because it deprived the state of the life of one of its citizens. If suicide was committed, punishment was severe: if done to avoid punishment for a crime, all of the person's real estate and personal property was forfeited to the king. A person who committed suicide to avoid bodily pain or in weariness of life lost only his personal property. People considered deranged or mentally retarded did not forfeit any property.

The American colonies adopted the same laws but rejected the severe penalties. Such penalties punished the relatives rather than the person who committed suicide. After the Revolutionary War, suicide was seldom prohibited by law and even more rarely punished. The only English penalty ever imposed in the colonies was a dishonorable burial. The person who committed suicide was denied a Christian burial. There are no recorded forfeitures of real estate or personal property in American colonial law.[51]

24. How has the law historically viewed assisted suicide and mercy killing?

Assisted suicide has been illegal in most states since the mid-eighteenth century when the practice was banned, either directly by statute or by court decision. Depending on the degree of assistance, assisting a suicide is often prosecuted as a form of homicide. Nearly one-half of the states allow the use of nondeadly force to thwart suicide attempts.[52]

As of this writing, thirty-four states explicitly prohibit assisted suicide by statute. The District of Columbia and twelve states (Alabama, Idaho, Maryland, Massachusetts, Michigan, North Carolina, Ohio, Nebraska, South Carolina, Vermont, Virginia, and West Virginia) criminalize assisted suicide through common law ("judge made" law). The status in another four states (Hawaii, Nevada, Utah, and Wyoming) is unclear because their courts and legislatures have never dealt with the issue. Finally, only one state, Oregon, permits physician-assisted suicide in limited circumstances, a measure which took effect in the fall of 1997.

The law has always considered acts of mercy killing to be homicide. The law does not accept the consent of the victim as a defense to a charge of homicide. Benevolent motive is not a legal excuse. As of this writing, forty-seven states expressly disapprove of mercy killing in their laws relating to natural death, living wills, or durable powers of attorney for health care.

25. What has the Supreme Court said about physician-assisted suicide?

In two landmark 1997 cases, the Supreme Court

for the first time ruled on assisted suicide. The Court unanimously upheld laws from New York and Washington States that prohibited physicians from assisting patients in killing themselves. In the first case, *Washington v. Glucksberg*, the Court determined that Washington's prohibition of assisted suicide did not violate the due process clause of the Constitution.[53]

To be a constitutionally protected, fundamental right and liberty, assisted suicide would need to be deeply rooted in this nation's history and tradition. The Court found no such tradition and said that this so-called right has been consistently rejected over time. More recently, state bans have been reexamined and generally reaffirmed. To find a constitutional right to assisted suicide would "reverse centuries of legal doctrine and practice, and strike down the considered policy choice of almost every State."[54]

Advocates of assisted suicide relied on the ten-year-old case of Nancy Cruzan, who existed in a permanently unconscious state following an automobile accident.[55] However, in *Cruzan*, the Court refused to hold that there is a constitutional right to die. Instead, the issue was the scope of the common-law doctrine of informed consent, which includes the right of a competent patient to refuse lifesaving nutrition and hydration.

The Supreme Court concluded in *Glucksberg* that bans on assisted suicide are rationally related to legitimate government interests, thereby meeting the least restrictive standard of constitutionality. Those important interests include (1) an "unqualified interest in the preservation of life," (2) an interest in protecting the integrity of the medical profession, and (3) an interest in protecting vulnerable groups. In other

49

words, the Supreme Court again did not find any right to die in the United States Constitution.

In *Vacco v. Quill*, the case from New York,[56] the Supreme Court unanimously agreed that New York's ban on assisted suicide does not violate the equal protection clause of the Fourteenth Amendment. The plaintiffs claimed it was discriminatory to permit withdrawal of life-supporting medical treatment, and at the same time prohibit physician-assisted suicide. However, the Court disagreed, stating there is a difference between withdrawal of treatment where the patient dies of the underlying injury or disease, and "killing" the patient with medication. Where the physician withdraws or withholds treatment, the *intent* is to relieve the burden of the dying process; the *intent* is not to cause death. The Court emphasized that there is no right to suicide or to hasten death. Such acts are different from the right to refuse treatment based on established rights to bodily integrity and freedom from unwanted touching.

The Court also examined the concern over the liberal use of painkillers at the end of life. Again, the Court distinguished acceptable intervention wherein the intent is not to cause death and the medical cause of death is the disease, from unacceptable intervention wherein the intended and actual medical cause of death is the intervention. In the words of the Court, "Painkilling drugs may hasten a patient's death, but the physician's purpose and intent is, or may be, only to ease his patient's pain."[57]

26. How does physician-assisted suicide become legal?

Physician-assisted suicide can be legalized in the

United States in one of three ways: (1) by a lower court decision, (2) by passage of a state law, or (3) by a Supreme Court decision that the action is a constitutional right. Although a few lower courts (trial and appellate courts) have recognized some form of physician-assisted suicide, these decisions have been rejected by higher courts. No court of final review has accepted physician-assisted suicide as a constitutional right. If the Supreme Court ever decides that there is a constitutional right to die, no state could prohibit assisted suicide or physician-assisted suicide. The state of Oregon is the only state as of this writing to take the initiative and legalize physician-assisted suicide in the absence of any such mandate from the Supreme Court.

27. How do countries outside the United States view physician-assisted suicide?

Only Colombia has declared physician-assisted suicide to be legal. On June 12, 1997, in a six to three decision, the Colombian Constitutional Court declared that, in accordance with the principles of the Magna Carta, euthanasia is permitted for terminally ill patients who give their express consent. The decision concluded that euthanasia would be permitted for individuals experiencing great pain, such as from AIDS, cancer, or renal deficiency, but not for degenerative illnesses such as Alzheimer's or Parkinson's disease. The Court left the legislature to deal with such issues as the manner of giving consent and the means of committing suicide. The liberal Court is considered an anomaly in this strongly conservative country.

The positive effect of the British opposition to physician-assisted suicide is seen in the great number of palliative care centers Great Britain has established in contrast to the Netherlands where physician-assisted suicide has been practiced for many years without penalty. This difference was duly noted by Justice Breyer at the January 8, 1997, oral argument in *Vacco v. Quill* and *Glucksberg v. Washington.*

Examples of other countries where significant decisions have been made include Canada and Australia. Physician-assisted suicide remains illegal in Canada after the 1993 *Rodriguez v. British Columbia* case.[58] The court upheld a criminal law against assisting or counseling another person to commit suicide. In Australia, the Northern Territory passed a law to permit physician-assisted suicide under narrowly prescribed circumstances. Fortunately, few physicians were willing to participate. A small number of instances of physician-assisted suicide occurred, but then the law was repealed.

28. What about euthanasia in the Netherlands?

Euthanasia (including various forms of assisted suicide) has not been legalized formally in the Netherlands. However, it is often excused, that is, not punished, under court-approved prosecutor guidelines. Efforts to change the law and to explicitly permit euthanasia failed. The judicial guidelines originally required a specific request from the person who sought death. Now, as a practical matter, the physicians make all the decisions, and this is generally tolerated.

Studies conducted in 1990 and 1995 reveal that 59 percent of Dutch physicians do not report their cases of assisted suicide and mercy killing. Also, more than 50 percent feel free to suggest euthanasia to their patients, and about 25 percent admit to ending patients' lives without their consent.[59]

In 1991, the Dutch Committee to Investigate the Medical Practice concerning Euthanasia reported that 10,615 patients' lives were terminated voluntarily, i.e., with patient consent. This total is the sum of figures in four subcategories: direct killing of patients (2,300 cases), provision of morphine in excessive doses with an intent to end life (3,159 cases), physician-assisted suicide (400 cases), and intentionally fatal withholding of life-prolonging treatment (4,756 cases). The committee also reported that 14,691 patients' lives were terminated involuntarily or nonvoluntarily, i.e., without expressed patient consent. This total is the sum of figures in three subcategories: direct killing of patients (1,000 cases), provision of morphine in excessive doses with an intent to end life (4,941 cases), and intentionally fatal withholding of life-prolonging treatment (8,750 cases). In the 1,000 cases of direct killing, 14 percent of the patients had complete mental capability and 11 percent had partial mental capability. In the 4,941 cases in which excessive amounts of morphine were administered, 27 percent of the patients had complete mental capability.[60] The Dutch experience demonstrates the futility of reliance on legal regulations to limit the practice of euthanasia. The guidelines established by Dutch courts have not been followed. The practice of euthanasia has moved from the terminally ill to the chronically ill, from those with physical illness to those patients with psychological distress, and from voluntary euthanasia to involuntary euthanasia.[61] It seems possible that our future concern may not be merely sliding down the slippery slope of euthanasia but falling off its precipice.

29. Would the legalization of assisted suicide justify it morally?

The legalization of assisted suicide does not justify it morally. Examples of the devastating consequences of legalizing an immoral act include the Supreme Court's 1857 *Dred Scott* decision that declared that no black person, free or slave, could claim United States citizenship, and the Court's decision in *Roe v. Wade* that in effect, legalized abortion throughout pregnancy. In the *Roe* decision, the Court contradicted years of legal, religious, and social objections to abortion. Many women, in the vulnerable position of contemplating an abortion they don't really want, rationalize that since the procedure is legal, it must also be moral.

It is the role of government to prohibit and punish behavior, hopefully based on moral considerations, but laws do not make the behavior moral or immoral. Morality is measured by a different standard, a higher standard, indeed, an absolute standard. If physician-assisted suicide gains judicial or legislative approval, more people will die at the hands of their physicians. They may think their choice is moral because it is within the bounds of the law. However, no government (especially one claiming in its oath of allegiance to be "under God") can delegate a power it does not possess, e.g., the power to intentionally take the life of another innocent human being.

30. How does the medical profession view the various forms of euthanasia?

The Hippocratic Oath and the practice of medicine based on it are committed to healing rather than killing, to life rather than death. Through the oath, physicians swear not to kill a patient or even to provide patients the means to kill themselves. The wishes of the patient are explicitly stated to be irrelevant in this matter.

Physicians, however, recognize that even were patients' true wishes to matter, they would be far from clear in the typical suicidal situation. Depression is frequently a factor that causes a person to pursue his or her own death. With treatment, however, depression may be diminished or cured.

Many different members of the medical profession are involved with suicidal patients. Normally, it is a family physician or a psychiatrist who has contact with the suicidal individual unless there is a suicide attempt; then emergency room personnel may be involved. In situations of terminal illness, there are often other specialists involved as well.

A 1994 American study of physician attitudes toward euthanasia published in the *New England Journal of Medicine* found that hematologists and oncologists had the most exposure to terminally ill patients and were the strongest opponents of physician-assisted suicide and euthanasia.[62] However, a study released in 1998, also published in *The New England Journal of Medicine*, suggests that this trend may be changing. Of the ten specialties surveyed, general internists and those who specialize in the care of the elderly and of lung problems were most likely to help hasten a patient's death.[63] At the time of this writing, the American Medical Association still opposes physician-assisted suicide; however, the current trend in medicine away from the principles of the Hippocratic Oath coupled with a lack of training among physicians to provide adequate palliative care is apparently encouraging a more tolerant attitude toward euthanasia.

31. Does suicide run in families?

Statistics show that those family members who are left in the wake of a suicide are at greater risk of committing suicide themselves. There is no single explanation for this, however, nor is there any certainty that suicide will strike a family more than once. Suicide is a choice made by individuals; it is not an infectious disease like smallpox or an inherited affliction like a genetic-based cancer. Although there may be contributing factors such as depression or schizophrenia that can have hereditary influences, there are also learned behavioral and social skills as well as personality traits and coping skills that can be a part of the explanation for suicide in families. Once suicide occurs in a family, it may also be seen by the surviving family members as an option for dealing with life's difficulties. Albeit, it is just as possible that a suicide in a family can be an antidote or deterrent for the family against future suicides because of the familial trauma it inflicts and the legacy it leaves.

No individual or family is predestined to suicide. If there has been a suicide in your family, you need not believe that the same tragedy will befall your family again. You should, however, be aware of the dynamics of suicide. At the same time, if your family has not experienced a suicide, there is no guarantee that it will continue to be free from such an act. Ultimately, suicide is always an individual and unfortunate act that brings immeasurable grief and devastation to families.

32. What is the suicide triangle?

The suicide triangle is a behavioral model for discussing the majority of suicides. In most suicides, there are three prominent elements: (1) an extremely humiliating experience or loss, (2) access to a firearm, and (3) the presence of alcohol. Many times when an individual experiences a great humiliation or a great loss (e.g., financial, familial, relational, or vocational), he or she turns to alcohol as a temporary comfort. Alcohol, however, is a depressant, and its consumption never enhances circumstances. Mixing alcohol with tragic circumstances often leads to further depression , and if there is ready access to a firearm, suicide may be the outcome. Just as oxygen, combustible materials, and a spark can produce a fire, so also can the suicide triangle of humiliating loss, alcohol, and a firearm produce a suicide.

This does not mean, of course, that every time these elements are present there will be a suicide nor that every suicide has these three elements. They are, however, common threads that run through many suicides. As such, we should be extremely sensitive to their *recurring* presence in our own lives and in the lives of those we love and cherish. Just as we say "don't drink and drive," so we must also try to separate these three elements (or any combination of them) whenever possible. It is particularly important to separate extreme or extended humiliation and access to lethal means (which can include means other than firearms, such as drugs). Even without alcohol there can be such hopelessness that there appears to be no way to resolve it except by suicide. The truth of the matter is that there is always a way to resolve hopelessness other than through suicide even though the solution may not be immediately apparent. Seek help. When you have suicidal thoughts, it is never wise to isolate yourself from others.

33. What are some of the warning signs that suggest a person may be considering suicide?

While we cannot predict suicide, there are some immediate danger signals to be aware of as we interact with others. The presence of these signals or warning signs do not necessarily mean that a person who displays them will attempt suicide, but they are very often strong indicators of suicidal thought. There are five distinct suicide danger signs[64]:

1. mental depression
2. marked changes in personality or behavior
3. making arrangements as though preparing for a final departure
4. suicide threats or other statements indicating a desire or intention to die
5. a suicide attempt

These five danger signs are communicated in a variety of ways and will vary from individual to individual. Among the things to look for are

- talk about wanting to die or to commit suicide
- a well-though-out plan of suicide
- withdrawal from friends and family
- changes in sleep patterns and/or appetite
- a sudden and extreme neglect of personal appearance
- decline in job or school performance or similar problems
- sudden change in personality and/or behavior
- aggressive and impulsive behavior such as violent outbursts
- prolonged depression over the recent death of a friend or relative
- drug or alcohol abuse
- talk about feeling worthless or being in hopeless circumstances
- giving away prized personal possessions
- sudden preparation of a will or review of insurance policies and estate papers
- unusual preoccupation or interest in the subject of death reflected in speech and letters or obsession with songs, books, or movies with suicidal themes

Not every person who is depressed, moody, or experiencing difficulty is suicidal. However, often after a suicide occurs, friends and family can see combinations of many of the indicators above. Any one of these is a cause for discussion, concern, and action, even if a person is not suicidal. If you have reason to think that someone is suicidal or might be suicidal (especially if there have been previous attempts or threats), intervention is crucial. Every suspicion of suicidal thought or behavior should be confronted immediately. The risk of embarrassment through acting in error is not nearly as great as the danger of the death of a friend, coworker, or loved one through the failure or hesitation to act.

In particular, spotting depression and getting help for those who are depressed is one way we can save lives. Depression is the psychological and emotional front door through which most suicidal people will pass. If we can meet them at the door, we can prevent much grief and many tragedies.

34. Can I still trust my physician if he or she accepts physician-assisted suicide as an alternative?

The physician-patient relationship is a very special and time-honored bond. Healing is the central purpose of medicine and of the physician's actions. The focus of the physician's energies should be on the patient, not on the family, the hospital, or any other party. It has been an accepted and understood premise of medicine that the patient's well-being should not be sacrificed to external pressures from other individuals, institutions, family members, or society. The sick receive care and treatment from the physician, not because they make claims or have desires, but because they are sick. They have needs. Thus, sickness and disease become a great leveling force in humanity and create dependence on the physician's skill, knowledge, and care. Any breech of this trust becomes critical.

Because of medical confidentiality, a patient would rarely, if ever, know that a physician has assisted in the suicide of another patient. So the relevant question is not, "Have you done it?" but, "Would you be willing to do it?" There are broader concerns, however, that arise simply if physician-assisted suicide becomes legal, whether or not patients know anything about their physicians' views on assisted suicide:

> The patient's trust in the doctor's wholehearted devotion to the patient's best interests will be hard to sustain once doctors are licensed to kill. . . . It will not matter that your doctor has never put anyone to death; that he is legally entitled to do so—even if only in some well-circumscribed areas—will make a world of difference. . . . And it will make a world of psychic difference too for conscientious physicians. How easily will they be able to care wholeheartedly for patients when it is always possible to think of killing them as a "therapeutic option?"[65]

Would most people's trust in their physicians really be affected? A recent survey of cancer patients suggests that it would. When asked about the possibility of physician-assisted suicide, most said that they would lose trust in a physician if the physician even mentioned physician-assisted suicide as an option. They also stated that they would change physicians if they knew that their physician had assisted in a suicide.[66]

The less we can trust the medical profession, the more we must rely on family (including church family) and friends. Making our wishes known to them verbally and in writing is the best means of gaining assurance that our final days and death will be honored and our life not cut short (see question on advance directives in *End of Life Decisions* in this series). Similar communication is also important with our physicians because they will usually respect patients' wishes regarding end-of-life care, even if they would personally prefer other options.

35. Is physician-assisted suicide the only alternative to fear of pain, fear of isolation, loss of control, and financial ruin?

The fear of isolation along with an indignation over increased reliance on medical technology often arouses the demand for a right to die and death with dignity. Leon Kass has identified the following fears that are common in the assertion of a right to die:

1. fear of prolongation of dying due to medical intervention; hence, the desire to refuse treatment or hospitalization, even if death occurs as a result
2. fear of living too long, without fatal illness to carry one off; hence, a desire for assisted suicide
3. fear of the degradations of senility and dependence; hence, the desire to die with dignity
4. fear of loss of control; hence, the desire to choose the time and manner of one's death
5. fear of becoming a burden to others—financial, psychic, social; hence the desire to die when one judges best[67]

Many of these fears are addressed elsewhere in this book (see especially the discussion of human dignity in question 15). Regardless of one's personal or family situation, there is much that health care and Christian faith have to offer. For example, the physician can relieve pain; provide strength, support, and comfort; avoid burdensome technologies that are likely to be futile; communicate with the patient and family;

and help to assign meaning to the patient's and family's suffering. The medical profession has never before been so capable of providing relief and comfort. To intentionally cause the death of a dying patient is an easy way for the physician to abandon these essential responsibilities.[68]

Health care, however, is more than just physician care. One of the greatest ways in which we can show care and compassion for the dying is by providing them with hospice care. Hospice care involves teams of nurses, chaplains, social workers, and others who aggressively relieve pain and ease suffering rather than continue useless, invasive treatments (see hospice question in *End of Life Decisions* in this series). Through hospice care, we can do much to alleviate the fears of the dying and also reduce the attractiveness of physician-assisted suicide. Hospice care gives assurance to the dying and their families that there will be dying with dignity.

There exists a highly developed program of support for those whose lives are threatened by incurable and end-stage illnesses. There is a specialized discipline of medicine focused on the relief of symptoms and maintenance of the highest level of function for the individual whose time is limited. There is a government-recognized, insurance-reimbursed program that provides support to patients, caregivers, and families. There is a service organization focused on whole-person-care, stressing life in the process of dying, with vast provisions to make that journey with integrity. There is hospice.[69]

There is also the church. Much of the support that dying people need has nothing to do with health care. They need a peace that transcends all understanding. That kind of peace comes from knowing that God will meet our deepest needs not only now but eternally. The church teaches and reminds us about this magnificent love and demonstrates it to us through selfless sharing. If you do not have such a church, by all means find one. It is God's great provision for the dying as well as the living (Heb. 10:19–25).

Many resources, then, are available to address the fears that accompany terminal illness and death. No one need turn to physician-assisted suicide as the only solution.

RELATIONAL MATTERS

36. What are the effects of suicide and physician-assisted suicide on surviving family and friends?

Suicide has a devastating impact on both individuals and families. Shock, anger, grief, fear, guilt, depression, shame, denial, self-recrimination, and confusion are among the many feelings in the aftermath of a suicide. Eric Marcus, who lost his father to suicide, writes: "The suicide of a loved one leaves in its wake a painful confusion that's expressed with a one-word question: *Why?* Embedded in that question are three others that begin with *why:* Why didn't we see it coming? Why didn't he/she come to us for help?

And above all else, Why did he/she do it?"[70] The search for answers and the vast array of emotions may continue for years, or even a lifetime. That is part of the tragedy of suicide: People commit suicide hoping to end pain and suffering, yet they inflict more trauma on their loved ones than ever anticipated.

The emotions are often heightened by the nature of the violent act of suicide. The loss of any friend or loved one brings grief and tears but even more so when the death is self-inflicted. No one is ever the same once they have been touched by suicide.

The impact on the family can be devastating. Again Eric Marcus laments:

> Just as suicide can devastate individuals, its impact on family—the complex web that includes brothers, sisters, parents, friends, uncles, aunts, and cousins—can be monumental. Some families are blown apart by the guilt and blame that can follow a suicide. Some are drawn together, rallying to support one another as they struggle through their individual and collective grief and confusion. Other families continue on in silence, pretending as best they can that nothing has happened or that the suicide was an accidental death.

In the case of my own family, my father's suicide blew apart already strained and fragile familial ties. My family has never recovered. I think of my father's suicide as an emotional bomb that he set off in our living room. No one was killed, but people were scattered in all directions and the emotional wreckage was everywhere.[71]

There can be healing and growth after a suicide, but like the physical scars we carry from wounds and injuries, suicide leaves an emotional scar that can never be fully eradicated.

The effects on friends and family when one has died through physician-assisted suicide can be different. In such cases there is still the grief of loss, but the questions of why may not be present. Because physician-assisted suicide is a controversial contemporary issue and not as prevalent as other suicides, there is not as much information available on the postsuicide ramifications. While some family members have expressed a sense of relief due to the removal of the pain and suffering from the deceased, the emotions involved are complex. People often wonder if there was something more they could have done—or why the care and support they provided was not enough to sustain the deceased. The more that people come to understand hospice care and the effectiveness of present-day pain management and the more that people learn about their availability, the worse those left behind after an assisted suicide will feel. Even when all friends and family agree with the assisted suicide in the first place, the long-term emotional damage may be immeasurable.

If you have lost someone you loved to suicide, it is important to know that there is hope. In Psalm 34:18 we read, "The LORD is near to the brokenhearted, and saves those who are crushed in spirit." In the midst of tears, trauma, and tragedy, Christians have the assurance that God will hear their prayers and petitions. God knows our emotions, our fears, and our circumstances and will be faithful to us if we will turn to him. Give yourself time to heal. It will be slow, but it will come. Don't be afraid to cry, for in your tears you will begin to recover. Remember that the choice that was made was not yours. You experience the pain, but you are not to blame for what has happened. You may never be the same again, but you can survive this tragedy and you can move beyond it. It need not remain at center stage in your life. Look to God for strength and help and know that He will give you sufficient grace for each day as you travel your new road.

37. What should I do if I feel suicidal or desire physician-assisted suicide?

If you are suicidal, talk with someone about your feelings and get appropriate medical and pastoral care immediately. Don't isolate yourself even though the tendency to do so will be strong. Find a friend, a family member, your pastor, your family physician, or a suicide hotline and talk. Feelings of loneliness, discouragement, depression, and hopelessness can be resolved. They are not permanent. There *is* hope. There *is* help. Your life is too important to God, to family members, and to friends for you to commit suicide.

Furthermore, avoid accepting belittling thoughts about yourself that can come to you when you are depressed or during times when you have experienced a setback. Negative thoughts should *only* serve as an impetus to change something about us for the better; they should motivate us to grow. Never should they be accepted as a commentary on what we will always be. Such destructive thoughts are the product of our fallen nature or the Devil (1 Peter 5:8). When we instead focus on God—who he is and what he can do—the possibilities for our future brighten considerably.

38. What should I do if I encounter someone whom I believe is suicidal or who indicates a desire for physician-assisted suicide?

If you think someone is suicidal, don't watch and wait. Talk to the individual. Listen to what he or she is saying. Don't be judgmental. Encourage the person to get help, and offer your assistance if you encounter reluctance. Don't use platitudes such as, "Cheer up!" and don't condemn or belittle the individual with statements such as, "that's dumb" or, "suicide's stupid." People who are considering suicide already feel bad and are generally aware that suicide is socially unacceptable. Listen to the person's conversation and solicit a promise that he or she won't attempt suicide "now," "today," or "tonight." If you are with the person, do not leave the individual alone. Don't hesitate to call for help or emergency services.

Remember, some people give warning signs if they are considering suicide (see question 34). These signs are calls for help and should receive a response from us. Tell the person you care, and then show the person that you care by assisting him or her to find help. The situation may well be one of life and death, and your response is critical. Moreover, only by your response will you be able to comfort yourself in the event that the individual you try to assist does eventually commit suicide. Although you would not be responsible for the suicide, your unwillingness to respond could produce feelings of intense personal guilt.

If you know someone is considering physician-assisted suicide, try to discover what the person has learned about his or her physical well-being that is so frightening. Fear of the unknown does not produce rational thinking. "Anxiety, depression, and a wish to die are the first reactions of many people who learn that they have a serious or deadly illness."[72] These patients are not significantly different from others who experience crises that seem too difficult to live with. The responsibility of a compassionate caregiver is to discover the patient's needs and provide the care that will meet them. Depression that often arises from receiving terrible news and the pain and frustration that often accompany disease and disability can be treated effectively.

People in crisis need assurance and hope. They also need to be encouraged to talk about their physical, emotional, mental, and spiritual concerns with their loved ones and friends. Though the tragedy is very personal to the patient, it is also very personal to the patient's loved ones and friends as well as others who may become involved in the patient's life as treatment and care progress.

Life is a challenge that throws many obstacles in our way, of which dying is but one. When these obstacles are faced rather than skirted, some good eventually comes, especially to those who love God (Rom. 8:28).

To choose assisted suicide at any time in the dying process robs everyone of the opportunity to resolve fears and repair or deepen precious relationships. Working through the dying process together with others provides a time to reflect on the most serious issues of life and death, some of which we too often neglect when we are healthy. Throughout life, which includes the experience of dying, sustain your faith in God, strengthen your hope in His promises, and deepen your love for others.

39. How should I respond to people who have attempted suicide?

With proper help, most people who are suicidal recover from their circumstances. Care and support from friends and family are crucial to this recovery. Much depends on your relationship with the person who has attempted suicide and his or her condition following the attempt. If you are a close friend or family member, you are in a good position to be supportive of the person's recovery in both the short and long term. The keys are to avoid making judgments and to *listen*. If it's appropriate, you can talk to the mental-health professionals, clergy, and others who are involved in caring for the person who has attempted suicide and learn how best you can be of help. You can also ask your loved one or family member directly, "What can I do to help you?" Another option is to call a suicide/crisis telephone line, explain your specific circumstances, and ask for suggestions on what you can do to help.[73]

Reaffirm to people who have attempted suicide your love and concern for them. Remind them of their value as human beings and of God's love for them. Pray for them and pray that you will have wisdom to help in their time of need. The majority of people who consider suicide should not be seen as mentally ill or crazy. Sometimes life's challenges are extremely taxing, and the burden of a load that gets heavier and heavier causes one to search for solutions. When a person comes to believe that solutions are not available, suicide becomes a possible and sometimes the only option. Our acceptance of those who struggle in life will help enable them to see the numerous solutions that feelings of hopelessness and despair too often gloss over. The burdens of another can usually be lightened by the assistance of a helping hand—yours!

40. How should I respond to someone close to me who has lost a loved one through suicide or physician-assisted suicide?

With any death, there will be tears and grief. In the case of a suicide, the loss is compounded. What can you do for someone you care for who is suffering from such a loss? Be present, be patient, be prayerful. People do not recover from the loss of loved ones quickly. You need to give them time to grieve. Most importantly, do not withdraw from them. Helping others who are grieving may feel awkward for you. However, if you hesitate or pull away, your absence will be noticed; your presence will be missed. Your presence, more than your words, is what is needed at this time. Be a good listener! Whether you convey your concern in person, by phone, or by letter, let the family know you care and are willing to help. Offer assistance and let them know that it is okay to talk about their loss with you. Don't assume that if they aren't talking everything is fine. Ask, "How are you doing?" or, "What would you like to talk about?"

The greatest mistake we can make is to pretend the death did not happen. It takes wisdom, discernment, and prayer to know when to speak and when not to speak (Eccl. 3:7b), but avoidance or denial is never the proper response. It is true that life goes on, but after a tragedy people need time to pick up life's pieces before they are able to move on effectively. If you are privileged to serve those who are grieving, you have been blessed with a great honor.

Conclusion

Ultimately, suicide is not about death but about living. The crises that push people toward suicide and physician-assisted suicide are real and should never be demeaned or diminished. But just as real are the solutions—medical, spiritual, and emotional.

As Christians, there are things we can do in response to suicidal individuals and our culture of death that is wrestling with physician-assisted suicide. We need to study the Scriptures and think very carefully about the nature of human life and the meaning of death. We need to think about the goodness of God, the sovereignty of God, and what it means to be created by God. Our lives are not our own but rather are a loan from God to manage wisely. We need to understand human suffering and how God uses it in our lives. We need to support the dying in better ways than we have in the past, and we need to encourage the medical community to continue to work in the field of pain management.

We also need to encourage our legislators to pass legislation that prohibits physician-assisted suicide, and we need to encourage the medical community to resist the practice of physician-assisted suicide. We need to pray for the dying, the discouraged, and those in distress that God will give them comfort and guidance. We need to pray for all those who practice medicine that they will do so with wisdom, skill, and commitment, upholding the oath to heal rather than kill. While we should oppose the most heinous forms of euthanasia as well, such as mercy killing, we need to recognize that the line must be drawn much earlier— i.e., before we embark down the path of assisted suicide—if killing people without their consent is to be avoided.

Remember: Assisted suicide is not an act of compassion. It is fundamentally at odds with biblical Christianity and is a misdirected attempt by a desperate culture to escape the hopelessness many experience when contemplating their own death. Christians have a critically important message for this generation. There is hope! Hope in Christ for life that surpasses this temporal existence.[74]

Throughout the pages of the Bible, the dignity and worth of every human life are emphasized repeatedly. So are the fallenness of the world and the reality of suffering. It is in enduring the latter without denying the former that we give glory to God. We also encourage others to respond appropriately to the challenges of dying.

The issues that we face as individuals and as a society are critical, and our responses have eternal as well as temporal ramifications. In all of our actions, we are to choose life, for regardless of the circumstances in which we find ourselves we can have the assurance of God's presence and love. For Christians, there is the promise and certainty that one day God "shall wipe away every tear from their eyes; and there shall no longer be any death; there shall no longer be any mourning, or crying, or pain" (Rev. 21:4). With

God's grace and strength, may we choose life in every circumstance until that day arrives.

> I have set before you life and death,
> the blessing and the curse.
> So *choose* life in order that you may live,
> you and your descendants,
> by loving the LORD your God,
> by obeying His voice,
> and by holding fast to Him;
> for this is your life and the length of your
> days. (Deut. 30:19–20, emphasis added)

Recommended Resources

The Center for Bioethics and Human Dignity Resources:

Brown, Harold O. J. et al. *Assisted Suicide and Euthanasia: A Christian Perspective Resource Notebook*, 1996.

Assisted Suicide and Euthanasia: A Christian Perspective: Supplemental Readings, 1996.

Cameron, Nigel M. de S. *Autonomy and the Right to Die*. Available in audio and video formats.

Kilner, John F., Arlene B. Miller, and Edmund D. Pellegrino. *Dignity and Dying: A Christian Appraisal.* Grand Rapids: Eerdmans, 1996.

Pellegrino, Edmund and Geoffrey Fieger. *A Public Debate on Legalizing Physician-Assisted Suicide*. Available in audio and video formats.

Other Resources:

Demy, Timothy J. and Gary P. Stewart, eds. *Suicide: A Christian Response: Crucial Considerations for Choosing Life.* Grand Rapids: Kregel, 1998.

Kilner, John F. *Life on the Line*. Grand Rapids: Eerdmans, 1992.

Mitsch, Raymond R. and Lynn Brookside. *Grieving the Loss of Someone You Love.* Ann Arbor, Mich.: Servant Publications, 1993.

Smith, Wesley J. *Forced Exit: The Slippery Slope from Assisted Suicide to Legalized Murder.* New York: Times Books, 1997.

Tada, Joni Eareckson. *When Is It Right to Die?* Grand Rapids: Zondervan, 1992.

Endnotes

1. E. S. Schneidman, *Definition of Suicide* (New York: Wiley, 1985), 203.

2. "Suicide Facts," Washington, D.C. National Institute of Mental Heath, 1995.

3. Judith M. Stillion and Eugene E. McDowell, *Suicide across the Life Span: Premature Exits*, 2d ed. (Washington, D.C.: Taylor and Friends, 1996), 98.

4. Ibid.

5. Matthew E. Conolly, "The Management of Cancer Pain," in *Suicide: A Christian Response, Crucial Considerations for Choosing Life*, ed. Timothy J. Demy and Gary P. Stewart (Grand Rapids: Kregel, 1998), 75.

6. Ibid., 94.

7. John F. Kilner, "Physician-Assisted Suicide: Today, Yesterday, and Tomorrow," in *Suicide: A Christian Response*, 152.

8. Peter J. Bernardi, *The Truth about Physician-Assisted Suicide* (Liguori, Mo.: Liguori Publications, 1996), 13.

9. See Robert J. Lifton, *The Nazi Doctors: Medical Killing and the Psychology of Genocide* (New York: Basic Books, 1995).

10. Richard L. Worsnop, "Care for the Dying," *The CQ Researcher* 7, no. 3 (September 1997): 776.

11. Diane E. Meier et. al., "A National Survey of Physician-Assisted Suicide and Euthanasia in the United States," *The New England Journal of Medicine* 338, no. 17 (April 1998): 1195.

12. Bernardi, *The Truth about Physician-Assisted Suicide*, 17.

13. Arthur J. Dyck, "Physician-Assisted Suicide: Is It Ethical?" *Harvard Divinity Bulletin* 21, no. 4 (1992): 17.

14. Robert D. Orr and Harold O. J. Brown, "Overview of the Key Issues," in *Assisted Suicide and Euthanasia: A Christian Perspective Resource Notebook,* ed. Harold O. J. Brown (Bannockburn, Ill.: Center for Bioethics and Human Dignity, 1996), 9.

15. Nigel M. de S. Cameron, "You Are Not Your Own," *Physician* (January-February 1997): 19.

16. Peter J. Bernardi, "Dr. Death's Dreadful Sermon," *Christianity Today,* 15 August 1994, 31.

17. Wesley J. Smith, *Forced Exit: The Slippery Slope from Assisted Suicide to Legalized Murder* (New York: Times Books, 1997), 210.

18. Edmund Pellegrino, "Euthanasia and Assisted Suicide," in *Dignity and Dying: A Christian Appraisal,* ed. John F. Kilner et. al. (Grand Rapids: Eerdmans, 1996), 118.

19. Paul Ramsey, "The Indignity of 'Death with Dignity,'" *Hastings Center Studies* 2 (May 1974): 48–49.

20. Pellegrino, "Euthanasia and Assisted Suicide," 113.

21. Hadley Arkes et al., "Always to Care, Never to Kill: A Declaration on Euthanasia," *First Things* (February 1992): 45.

22. Stillion and McDowell, *Suicide Across the Life Span,* 17–20.

23. "Suicide Facts."

24. Stillion and McDowell, *Suicide Across the Life Span,* 19.

25. Eric Marcus, *Why Suicide?* (San Francisco: HarperCollins, 1996), 2.

26. "Suicide Facts."

27. Marcus, *Why Suicide?,* 28–29.

28. Worsnop, "Caring for the Dying," 780. See also Henk Jochemsen, "The Netherlands Experiment" in *Dignity and Dying: A Christian Appraisal,* 165–79.

29. Smith, *Forced,* 99.

30. Meier et. al., "A National Survey of Physician-Assisted Suicide and Euthanasia in the United States," 1200.

31. Pellegrino, "Euthanasia and Assisted Suicide," 113.
32. Leon R. Kass, "Death With Dignity and the Sanctity of Life," *Commentary* (March 1990): 43.
33. It is debated as to whether or not the death of Samson, recorded in Judges 16, was a suicide. It might be viewed as an act in which he knew he would probably die, but in which death was not the intent. The intent was the defeat of his enemies.
34. See Eugene H. Merrill, "Suicide and the Concept of Death in the Old Testament," and Dónal P. O'Mathúna, "But the Bible Doesn't Say They Were Wrong to Commit Suicide, Does It?" in *Suicide: A Christian Response*, 315–26 and 349–66 respectively.
35. Merrill, "Suicide and the Concept of Death in the Old Testament," 323.
36. Ibid.
37. Dónal P. O'Mathúna, "Did Paul Condone Suicide?" in *Suicide: A Christian Response*, 395.
38. See J. Daryl Charles, "The 'Right to Die' in the Light of Contemporary Rights-Rhetoric," in *Bioethics and the Future of Medicine: A Christian Appraisal*, ed. John F. Kilner, Nigel M. de S. Cameron, and David L. Schiedermayer (Grand Rapids: Eerdmans, 1995), 263–79.
39. Charles P. Arand, "Personal Autonomy Versus Creaturely Contingency: The First Article and the Right to Die," *Concordia Journal* 20 (December 1994): 386–87.
40. Leon R. Kass, "Is There a Right to Die?" *Hastings Center Report* (January–February 1993): 36.
41. Ibid., 38.
42. Ibid., 42.
43. Ibid. See also, Nigel Cameron, "Autonomy and the Right to Die," in *Dignity and Dying*, 23–33.
44. For a very helpful discussion see John F. Kilner, "Forgoing Treatment," in *Dignity and Dying*, 69–83.
45. Ibid., 78.

46. Matthew R. Conolly, "The Management of Cancer Pain," in *Suicide: A Christian Response*, 97.

47. Pellegrino, "Euthanasia and Assisted Suicide," 115.

48. Ibid., 112.

49. Stanley Hauerwas, "Rational Suicide and Reasons for Living," in *On Moral Medicine: Theological Perspectives in Euthanasia*, ed. Stephen Lammers and Allen Verhey (Grand Rapids: Eerdmans, 1987), 465.

50. Darrel W. Amundsen, "Did Early Christians 'Lust After Death'?" in *Suicide: A Christian Response*, 292–93.

51. Edward R. Grant and Paul Benjamin Linton, "Relief or Reproach?: Euthanasia Rights in the Wake of Measure 16," *Oregon L. Rev.* 74 (1995): 449, 481–87.

52. Ibid., 483–85.

53. *Washington v. Glucksberg*, 65 U.S.L.W. 4664 (U.S. June 26, 1997).

54. *Cruzan v. Director, Mo. Dept. of Health*, 497 U.S. 261 (1990).

55. Ibid.

56. *Vacco v. Quill*, 65 U.S.L.W. 4695 (June 26, 1997).

57. Ibid.

58. *Rodriguez v. British Columbia*, 107 D.L.R. 4th 342 (1993).

59. Hendin et. al, *JAMA* (June 1997): 1722.

60. Richard Fenigsen, "The Report of the Dutch Governmental Committee on Euthanasia," *Issues in Law and Medicine 7 (Winter 1991): 339–44.*

61. Herbert Hendin, "Physician-Assisted Suicide: What Next?" *The Responsive Community: Rights and Responsibilities* 7, no. 4 (Fall 1997): 24–32.

62. J. S. Cohen et. al., "Attitudes toward Assisted Suicide and Euthanasia among Physicians in Washington State," *The New England Journal of Medicine* 331 (July 1994): 93.

63. Meier, et. al., "A National Survey of Physician-Assisted Suicide and Euthanasia in the United States."

64. American Association of Suicidology, *Suicide and How to Prevent It,* nd., 4.

65. Kass, "Neither for Love Nor Money: Why Doctors Must Not Kill," *The Public Interest* 94 (Winter 1989): 35.

66. "Attitudes toward Euthanasia Sharply Divide, Survey Finds," *Reuthers*, 29 June 1996, cited in Smith, *Forced Exit,* 5.

67. Kass, "Is There a Right to Die?", 37.

68. William Reichel and Arthur J. Dyck, "Euthanasia: A Contemporary Moral Quandary," *Lancet* 2, no. 8675 (December 1989): 1322.

69. Martha L. Twaddle, "Hospice Care," in *Dignity and Dying,* 184.

70. Marcus, *Why Suicide?*, 128.

71. Ibid., 134.

72. Herbert Hendin, "Physician-Assisted Suicide: What Next?", 22–24.

73. Marcus, *Why Suicide?*, 97.

74. C. Ben Mitchell, "Physician-Assisted Suicide and the Great Physician," in *Assisted Suicide and Euthanasia: A Christian Perspective Resource Notebook,* ed. Harold O. J. Brown et. al. (Bannockburn, Ill.: Center for Bioethics and Human Dignity, 1996), 26.